Annus Mirabilis; The Year of Wonders, 1666 by John Dryden

AN HISTORICAL POEM

John Dryden was born on August 9th, 1631 in the village rectory of Aldwincle near Thrapston in Northamptonshire. As a boy Dryden lived in the nearby village of Titchmarsh, Northamptonshire. In 1644 he was sent to Westminster School as a King's Scholar.

Dryden obtained his BA in 1654, graduating top of the list for Trinity College, Cambridge that year.

Returning to London during The Protectorate, Dryden now obtained work with Cromwell's Secretary of State, John Thurloe.

At Cromwell's funeral on 23 November 1658 Dryden was in the company of the Puritan poets John Milton and Andrew Marvell. The setting was to be a sea change in English history. From Republic to Monarchy and from one set of lauded poets to what would soon become the Age of Dryden.

The start began later that year when Dryden published the first of his great poems, Heroic Stanzas (1658), a eulogy on Cromwell's death.

With the Restoration of the Monarchy in 1660 Dryden celebrated in verse with Astraea Redux, an authentic royalist panegyric.

With the re-opening of the theatres after the Puritan ban, Dryden began to also write plays. His first play, The Wild Gallant, appeared in 1663 but was not successful. From 1668 on he was contracted to produce three plays a year for the King's Company, in which he became a shareholder. During the 1660s and '70s, theatrical writing was his main source of income.

In 1667, he published Annus Mirabilis, a lengthy historical poem which described the English defeat of the Dutch naval fleet and the Great Fire of London in 1666. It established him as the pre-eminent poet of his generation, and was crucial in his attaining the posts of Poet Laureate (1668) and then historiographer royal (1670).

This was truly the Age of Dryden, he was the foremost English Literary figure in Poetry, Plays, translations and other forms.

In 1694 he began work on what would be his most ambitious and defining work as translator, The Works of Virgil (1697), which was published by subscription. It was a national event.

John Dryden died on May 12th, 1700, and was initially buried in St. Anne's cemetery in Soho, before being exhumed and reburied in Westminster Abbey ten days later.

Index of Contents

AN ACCOUNT OF THE ENSUING POEM, IN A LETTER TO THE HON. SIR ROBERT HOWARD.
ANNUS MIRABILIS; THE YEAR OF WONDERS, 1666. VERSES I - CCCIV
JOHN DRYDEN – A SHORT BIOGRAPHY
JOHN DRYDEN – A CONCISE BIBLIOGRAPHY

TO THE METROPOLIS OF GREAT-BRITAIN, THE MOST RENOWNED AND LATE FLOURISHING
CITY OF LONDON, IN ITS REPRESENTATIVES, THE LORD-MAYOR AND COURT OF ALDERMEN, THE
SHERIFFS, AND COMMON-COUNCIL OF IT.

As, perhaps, I am the first who ever presented a work of this nature to the metropolis of any nation, so it is likewise consonant to justice, that he, who was to give the first example of such a dedication, should begin it with that city, which has set a pattern to all others, of true loyalty, invincible courage, and unshaken constancy. Other cities have been praised for the same virtues, but I am much deceived if any have so dearly purchased their reputation: their fame has been won them by cheaper trials than an expensive, though necessary war, a consuming pestilence, and a more consuming fire. To submit yourselves with that humility to the judgments of heaven, and, at the same time, to raise yourselves with that vigour above all human enemies; to be combated at once from above, and from below; to be struck down, and to triumph,--I know not whether such trials have been ever paralleled in any nation: the resolution and successes of them never can be. Never had prince or people more mutual reason to love each other, if suffering for each other can endear affection. You have come together a pair of matchless lovers, through many difficulties; he, through a long exile, various traverses of fortune, and the interposition of many rivals, who violently ravished and with-held you from him; and certainly you have had your share in sufferings. But providence has cast upon you want of trade, that you might appear bountiful to your country's necessities; and the rest of your afflictions are not more the effects of God's displeasure (frequent examples of them having been in the reign of the most excellent princes) than occasions for the manifesting of your christian and civil virtues. To you, therefore, this Year of Wonders is justly dedicated, because you have made it so; you, who are to stand a wonder to all years and ages; and who have built yourselves an immortal monument on your own ruins. You are now a Phœnix in her ashes, and, as far as humanity can approach, a great emblem of the suffering Deity; but heaven never made so much piety and virtue to leave it miserable. I have heard, indeed, of some virtuous persons who have ended unfortunately, but never of any virtuous nation: Providence is engaged too deeply, when the cause becomes so general; and I cannot imagine it has resolved that ruin of the people at home, which it has blessed abroad with such successes. I am therefore to conclude, that your sufferings are at an end; and that one part of my poem has not been more an history of your destruction, than the other a prophecy of your restoration. The accomplishment of which happiness, as it is the wish of all true Englishmen, so is it by none more passionately desired, than by

The greatest of your admirers,
And most humble of your servants,
JOHN DRYDEN.

AN ACCOUNT OF THE ENSUING POEM, IN A LETTER TO THE HON. SIR ROBERT HOWARD.

SIR,

I am so many ways obliged to you, and so little able to return your favours, that, like those who owe too much, I can only live by getting farther into your debt. You have not only been careful of my fortune, which was the effect of your nobleness, but you have been solicitous of my reputation, which is that of your kindness. It is not long since I gave you the trouble of perusing a play for me, and now, instead of an acknowledgment, I have given you a greater, in the correction of a poem. But since you are to bear this persecution, I will at least give you the encouragement of a martyr,--you could never suffer in a nobler cause; for I have chosen the most heroic subject, which any poet could desire. I have taken upon me to describe the motives, the beginning, progress, and successes, of a most just and necessary war; in it, the care, management, and prudence of our king; the conduct and valour of a royal admiral, and of two incomparable generals; the invincible courage of our captains and seamen; and three glorious victories, the result of all. After this, I have, in the Fire, the most deplorable, but withal the greatest, argument that can be imagined; the destruction being so swift, so sudden, so vast and miserable, as nothing can parallel in story. The former part of this poem, relating to the war, is but a due expiation for my not serving my king and country in it. All gentlemen are almost obliged to it; and I know no reason we should give that advantage to the commonalty of England, to be foremost in brave actions, which the nobles of France would never suffer in their peasants. I should not have written this but to a person, who has been ever forward to appear in all employments, whither his honour and generosity have called him. The latter part of my poem, which describes the Fire, I owe, first, to the piety and fatherly affection of our monarch to his suffering subjects; and, in the second place, to the courage, loyalty, and magnanimity of the city; both which were so conspicuous, that I have wanted words to celebrate them as they deserve. I have called my poem historical, not epic, though both the actions and actors are as much heroic as any poem can contain. But, since the action is not properly one, nor that accomplished in the last successes, I have judged it too bold a title for a few stanzas, which are little more in number than a single Iliad, or the longest of the Æneids. For this reason, (I mean not of length, but broken action, tied too severely to the laws of history) I am apt to agree with those, who rank Lucan rather among historians in verse, than Epic poets; in whose room, if I am not deceived, Silius Italicus, though a worse writer, may more justly be admitted. I have chosen to write my poem in quatrains, or stanzas of four in alternate rhyme, because I have ever judged them more noble, and of greater dignity, both for the sound and number, than any other verse in use amongst us; in which I am sure I have your approbation. The learned languages have certainly a great advantage of us, in not being tied to the slavery of any rhyme; and were less constrained in the quantity of every syllable, which they might vary with spondees or dactyls, besides so many other helps of grammatical figures, for the lengthening or abbreviation of them, than the modern are in the close of that one syllable, which often confines, and more often corrupts, the sense of all the rest. But in this necessity of our rhymes, I have always found the couplet verse most easy, (though not so proper for this occasion,) for there the work is sooner at an end, every two lines concluding the labour of the poet; but in quatrains he is to carry it farther on, and not only so, but to bear along in his head the troublesome sense of four lines together. For, those, who write correctly in this kind, must needs acknowledge, that the last line of the stanza is to be considered in the composition of the first. Neither can we give ourselves the liberty of making any part of a verse for the sake of rhyme, or concluding with a word which is not current English, or using the variety of female rhymes, all which our fathers practised; and for the female rhymes, they are still in use amongst other nations; with the Italian in every line, with the Spaniard promiscuously, with the French alternately, as those who have read the Alaric, the Pucelle, or any of their later poems, will agree with me. And besides this, they write in Alexandrines, or verses of six feet; such as, amongst us, is the old translation of Homer by Chapman: all which, by lengthening of their chain, makes the sphere of their activity the larger.

I have dwelt too long upon the choice of my stanza, which you may remember is much better defended in the preface to "Gondibert;" and therefore I will hasten to acquaint you with my endeavours in the writing. In general I will only say, I have never yet seen the description of any naval fight in the proper terms which are used at sea; and if there be any such, in another language, as that of Lucan in the third of his Pharsalia, yet I could not avail myself of it in the English; the terms of art in every tongue bearing more of the idiom of it than any other words. We hear indeed among our poets, of the thundering of guns, the smoke, the disorder, and the slaughter; but all these are common notions. And certainly, as those, who in a logical dispute keep in general terms, would hide a fallacy; so those, who do it in any poetical description, would veil their ignorance:

_Descriptas servare vices, operumque colores,
Cur ego, si nequeo ignoroque, poeta salutor?_

For my own part, if I had little knowledge of the sea, yet I have thought it no shame to learn; and if I have made some few mistakes, it is only, as you can bear me witness, because I have wanted opportunity to correct them; the whole poem being first written, and now sent you from a place, where I have not so much as the converse of any seaman. Yet though the trouble I had in writing it was great, it was more than recompensed by the pleasure. I found myself so warm in celebrating the praises of military men, two such especially as the prince and general, that it is no wonder if they inspired me with thoughts above my ordinary level. And I am well satisfied, that, as they are incomparably the best subject I ever had, excepting only the royal family, so also, that this I have written of them is much better than what I have performed on any other. I have been forced to help out other arguments, but this has been bountiful to me; they have been low and barren of praise, and I have exalted them, and made them fruitful; but here--_Omnia sponte suà reddit justissima tellus_. I have had a large, a fair, and a pleasant field; so fertile, that, without my cultivating, it has given me two harvests in a summer, and in both oppressed the reaper. All other greatness in subjects is only counterfeit; it will not endure the test of danger; the greatness of arms is only real. Other greatness burdens a nation with its weight; this supports it with its strength. And as it is the happiness of the age, so it is the peculiar goodness of the best of kings, that we may praise his subjects without offending him. Doubtless it proceeds from a just confidence of his own virtue, which the lustre of no other can be so great as to darken in him; for the good or the valiant are never safely praised under a bad or a degenerate prince.

But to return from this digression to a farther account of my poem; I must crave leave to tell you, that as I have endeavoured to adorn it with noble thoughts, so much more to express those thoughts with elocution. The composition of all poems is, or ought to be, of wit; and wit in the poet, or wit-writing, (if you will give me leave to use a school-distinction) is no other than the faculty of imagination in the writer, which, like a nimble spaniel, beats over and ranges through the field of memory, 'till it springs the quarry it hunted after; or, without metaphor, which searches over all the memory for the species or ideas of those things, which it designs to represent. Wit written is that which is well defined, the happy result of thought, or product of imagination. But to proceed from wit, in the general notion of it, to the proper wit of an Heroic or Historical Poem, I judge it chiefly to consist in the delightful imagining of persons, actions, passions, or things. It is not the jerk or sting of an epigram, nor the seeming contradiction of a poor antithesis, (the delight of an ill-judging audience in a play of rhyme,) nor the gingle of a more poor paronomasia; neither is it so much the morality of a grave sentence, affected by Lucan, but more sparingly used by Virgil; but it is some lively and apt description, dressed in such colours of speech, that it sets before your eyes the absent object, as perfectly, and more delightfully than nature. So then the first happiness of the poet's imagination is properly invention, or finding of the thought; the second is fancy, or the variation, deriving, or moulding, of that thought, as the judgment represents it proper to the subject; the third is elocution, or the art of clothing and adorning that thought, so found and varied, in apt, significant, and sounding words. The quickness of the imagination is seen in the invention, the fertility in the fancy, and the accuracy in the expression. For the two first of these, Ovid is famous amongst the poets; for the latter, Virgil. Ovid images more often the movements and affections of the mind, either combating between two contrary passions, or extremely discomposed by one. His words therefore are the least part of his care; for he pictures nature in disorder, with which the study and choice of words is inconsistent. This is the proper wit of dialogue or discourse, and consequently of the drama, where all that is said is supposed to be the effect of sudden thought; which, though it excludes not the quickness of wit in repartees, yet admits not a too curious election of words, too frequent allusions, or use of tropes, or, in fine, any thing that shews remoteness of thought, or labour in the writer. On the other side, Virgil speaks not so often to us in the person of another, like Ovid, but in his own: he relates almost all things as from himself, and thereby gains more liberty than the other, to express his thoughts with all the graces of elocution, to write more figuratively, and to confess as well the labour as the force of his imagination. Though he describes his Dido well and naturally, in the violence of her passions, yet he must yield in that to the Myrrha, the Biblis, the Althæa, of Ovid; for, as great an admirer of him as I am, I must acknowledge, that if I see not more of their souls than I see of Dido's, at least I have a greater concernment for them: and that convinces me, that Ovid has touched those tender strokes more delicately than Virgil could. But when action or persons are to be described, when any such image is to be set before us, how bold, how masterly, are the strokes of Virgil! We see the objects he presents us with in their native figures, in their proper motions; but so we see them, as our own eyes could never have beheld them so beautiful in themselves. We see the soul of the poet, like that universal one of which he speaks, informing and moving through all his pictures:

--Totamque infusa per artus
Mens agitat molem, et magno se corpore miscet._

We behold him embellishing his images, as he makes Venus breathing beauty upon her son Æneas:

--lumenque juventæ
Purpureum, & lætos oculis afflârat honores:
Quale manus addunt ebori decus, aut ubi flavo
Argentum, Pariusve lapis, circundatur auro._

See his Tempest, his Funeral Sports, his Combat of Turnus and Æneas: and in his "Georgics," which I esteem the divinest part of all his writings, the Plague, the Country, the Battle of the Bulls, the labour of the Bees; and those many other excellent images of nature, most of which are neither great in themselves, nor have any natural ornament to bear them up; but the words wherewith he describes them are so excellent, that it might be well applied to him, which was said by Ovid, _Materium superabat opus_: the very sound of his words has often somewhat that is connatural to the subject; and while we read him, we sit, as in a play, beholding the scenes of what he represents. To perform this, he made frequent use of tropes, which you know change the nature of a known word, by applying it to some other signification; and this is it which Horace means in his Epistle to the Piso's:

_Dixeris egregiè, notum si callida verbum
Reddiderit junctura novum._----

But I am sensible I have presumed too far to entertain you with a rude discourse of that art, which you both know so well, and put into practice with so much happiness. Yet before I leave Virgil, I must own the vanity to tell you, and by you the world, that he has been my master in this poem. I have followed him every where, I know not with what success, but I am sure with diligence enough; my images are many of them copied from him, and the rest are imitations of him. My expressions also are as near as the idioms of the two languages would admit of in translation. And this, sir, I have done with that boldness, for which I will stand accountable to any of our little critics, who, perhaps, are no better acquainted with him than I am. Upon your first perusal of this poem, you have taken notice of some words, which I have innovated (if it be too bold for me to say refined) upon his Latin; which, as I offer not to introduce into English prose, so I hope they are neither improper, nor altogether inelegant in verse; and, in this, Horace will again defend me:

_Et nova, fictaque nuper, habebunt verba fidem, si
Græco fonte cadunt, parcè detorta._----

The inference is exceeding plain; for, if a Roman poet might have liberty to coin a word, supposing only that it was derived from the Greek, was put into a Latin termination, and that he used this liberty but seldom, and with modesty; how much more justly may I challenge that privilege to do it with the same prerequisites, from the best and most judicious of Latin writers? In some places, where either the fancy or the words were his, or any other's, I have noted it in the margin, that I might not seem a plagiary; in others I have neglected it, to avoid as well tediousness, as the affectation of doing it too often. Such descriptions or images well wrought, which I promise not for mine, are, as I have said, the adequate delight of heroic poesy; for they beget admiration, which is its proper object; as the images of the burlesque, which is contrary to this, by the same reason beget laughter: for, the one shews nature beautified, as in the picture of a fair woman, which we all admire; the other shews her deformed, as in that of a lazar, or of a fool with distorted face and antique gestures, at which we cannot forbear to laugh, because it is a deviation from nature. But though the same images serve equally for the Epic poesy, and for the Historic and Panegyric, which are branches of it, yet a several sort of sculpture is to be used in them. If some of them are to be like those of Juvenal, _stantes in curribus Æmiliani_, heroes drawn in their triumphal chariots, and in their full proportion; others are to be like that of Virgil, _spirantia mollius æra_: there is somewhat more of softness and tenderness to be shewn in them. You will soon find I write not this without concern. Some, who have seen a paper of verses, which I wrote last year to her highness the Duchess, have accused them of that only thing I could defend in them. They said, I did _humi serpere_,--that I wanted not only height of fancy, but dignity of words, to set it off. I might well answer with that of Horace, _Nunc non erat his locus_; I knew I addressed them to a lady, and accordingly I affected the softness of expression, and the smoothness of measure, rather than the height of thought; and in what I did endeavour, it is no vanity to say I have succeeded. I detest arrogance; but there is some difference betwixt that and a just defence. But I will not farther bribe your candour, or the reader's. I leave them to speak for me; and, if they can, to make out that character, not pretending to a greater, which I have given them.

And now, sir, it is time I should relieve you from the tedious length of this account. You have better and more profitable employment for your hours, and I wrong the public to detain you longer. In conclusion, I must leave my poem to you with all its faults, which I hope to find fewer in the printing by your emendations. I know you are not of the number of those, of whom the younger Pliny speaks; _Nec sunt parum multi, qui carpere amicos suos judicium vocant_: I am rather too secure of you on that side. Your candour in pardoning my errors may make you more remiss in correcting them; if you will not withal consider, that they come into the world with your approbation, and through your hands. I beg from you the greatest favour you can confer upon an absent person, since I repose upon your management what is dearest to me, my fame and reputation; and therefore I hope it will stir you up to make my poem fairer by many of your blots: if not, you know the story of the gamester who married the rich man's daughter, and when her father denied the portion, christened all the children by his sirname, that if, in conclusion, they must beg, they should do so by one name, as well as by the other. But, since the reproach of my faults will light on you, it is but reason I should do you that justice to the readers, to let them know, that, if there be any thing tolerable in this poem, they owe the argument to your choice, the writing to your encouragement, the correction to your judgment, and the care of it to your friendship, to which he must ever acknowledge himself to owe all things, who is,

SIR,
The most obedient, and most
Faithful of your servants,
JOHN DRYDEN.

From Charlton, in Wiltshire,
Nov. 10, 1666.

ANNUS MIRABILIS; THE YEAR OF WONDERS, 1666.

I
In thriving arts long time had Holland grown,
Crouching at home and cruel when abroad;
Scarce leaving us the means to claim our own;
Our king they courted, and our merchants awed.[98]

II
Trade, which like blood should circularly flow,
Stopped in their channels, found its freedom lost;
Thither the wealth of all the world did go,
And seemed but shipwrecked on so base a coast.

III
For them alone the heavens had kindly heat,
In eastern quarries ripening precious dew;[99]
For them the Idumæan balm did sweat,
And in hot Ceylon spicy forests grew.

IV
The sun but seemed the labourer of the year;
Each waxing moon supplied her watery store,[100]
To swell those tides, which from the Line did bear
Their brim-full vessels to the Belgian shore.

V
Thus, mighty in her ships, stood Carthage long,
And swept the riches of the world from far;
Yet stooped to Rome, less wealthy, but more strong;

And this may prove our second Punic war.[101]

VI

What peace can be, where both to one pretend?
(But they more diligent, and we more strong,)
Or if a peace, it soon must have an end;
For they would grow too powerful, were it long.

VII

Behold two nations then, engaged so far,
That each seven years the fit must shake each land;
Where France will side to weaken us by war,
Who only can his vast designs withstand.

VIII

See how he feeds the Iberian[102] with delays,
To render us his timely friendship vain;
And while his secret soul on Flanders preys,
He rocks the cradle of the babe of Spain.[103]

IX

Such deep designs of empire does he lay
O'er them, whose cause he seems to take in hand;
And prudently would make them lords at sea,
To whom with ease he can give laws by land.

X

This saw our king; and long within his breast
His pensive counsels balanced to and fro;
He grieved the land he freed should be oppressed,
And he less for it than usurpers do.[104]

XI

His generous mind the fair ideas drew
Of fame and honour, which in dangers lay;
Where wealth, like fruit on precipices, grew,
Not to be gathered but by birds of prey.

XII

The loss and gain each fatally were great;
And still his subjects called aloud for war:
But peaceful kings, o'er martial people set,
Each other's poize and counterbalance are.

XIII

He first surveyed the charge with careful eyes,
Which none but mighty monarchs could maintain;
Yet judged, like vapours that from limbecks rise,

It would in richer showers descend again.

XIV

At length resolved to assert the watery ball,
He in himself did whole Armadas bring;
Him aged seamen might their master call,
And chuse for general, were he not their king.[105]

XV

It seems as every ship their sovereign knows,
His awful summons they so soon obey;--
So hear the scaly herd when Proteus blows,
And so to pasture follow through the sea.[106]

XVI

To see this fleet upon the ocean move,
Angels drew wide the curtains of the skies;
And heaven, as if there wanted lights above,
For tapers made two glaring comets rise.[107]

XVII

Whether they unctuous exhalations are,
Fired by the sun, or seeming so alone;
Or each some more remote and slippery star,
Which loses footing when to mortals shewn;

XVIII

Or one, that bright companion of the sun,[108]
Whose glorious aspect sealed our new-born king;
And now, a round of greater years begun,
New influence from his walks of light did bring.

XIX

Victorious York did first, with famed success,
To his known valour make the Dutch give place;[109]
Thus heaven our monarch's fortune did confess,
Beginning conquest from his royal race.

XX

But since it was decreed, auspicious king,
In Britain's right that thou shouldst wed the main,
Heaven, as a gage, would cast some precious thing,
And therefore doomed that Lawson should be slain.[110]

XXI

Lawson amongst the foremost met his fate,
Whom sea-green Sirens from the rocks lament;
Thus, as an offering for the Grecian state,

He first was killed, who first to battle went.[111]

XXII

Their chief blown up, in air, not waves, expired,
To which his pride presumed to give the law;[112]
The Dutch confessed heaven present, and retired,
And all was Britain the wide ocean saw.

XXIII

To nearest ports their shattered ships repair,
Where by our dreadful cannon they lay awed;
So reverently men quit the open air,
Where thunder speaks the angry gods abroad.

XIV

And now approached their fleet from India, fraught
With all the riches of the rising sun;
And precious sand from southern climates brought,
The fatal regions where the war begun.[113]

XXV

Like hunted castors, conscious of their store,[114]
Their way-laid wealth to Norway's coast they bring;
There first the North's cold bosom spices bore,
And winter brooded on the eastern spring.

XXVI

By the rich scent we found our perfumed prey,
Which, flanked with rocks, did close in covert lie;
And round about their murdering cannon lay,
At once to threaten and invite the eye.

XXVII

Fiercer than cannon, and than rocks more hard,
The English undertake the unequal war;
Seven ships alone, by which the port is barred,
Besiege the Indies, and all Denmark dare.

XXVIII

These fight like husbands, but like lovers those;
These fain would keep, and those more fain enjoy;
And to such height their frantic passion grows,
That what both love, both hazard to destroy.

XXIX

Amidst whole heaps of spices lights a ball,
And now their odours armed against them fly;
Some preciously by shattered porcelain fall,

And some by aromatic splinters die.

XXX
And though by tempests of the prize bereft,
In heaven's inclemency some ease we find;
Our foes we vanquished by our valour left,
And only yielded to the seas and wind.

XXXI
Nor wholly lost we so deserved a prey;
For storms, repenting, part of it restored;
Which as a tribute from the Baltic sea,
The British ocean sent her mighty lord.[115]

XXXII
Go, mortals, now, and vex yourselves in vain
For wealth, which so uncertainly must come;
When what was brought so far, and with such pain,
Was only kept to lose it nearer home.

XXXIII
The son, who twice three months on th' ocean tost,
Prepared to tell what he had passed before,
Now sees in English ships the Holland coast,
And parents' arms, in vain, stretched from the shore.

XXXIV
This careful husband had been long away,
Whom his chaste wife and little children mourn;
Who on their fingers learned to tell the day,
On which their father promised to return.

XXXV
Such are the proud designs of human-kind,
And so we suffer shipwreck every where![116]
Alas, what port can such a pilot find,
Who in the night of fate must blindly steer!

XXXVI
The undistinguished seeds of good and ill,
Heaven in his bosom from our knowledge hides;
And draws them in contempt of human skill,
Which oft, for friends mistaken, foes provides.

XXXVII
Let Munster's prelate ever be accurst,
In whom we seek the German faith in vain;[117]
Alas, that he should teach the English first,

That fraud and avarice in the church could reign!

XXXVIII
Happy, who never trust a stranger's will,
Whose friendship's in his interest understood;
Since money given but tempts him to be ill,
When power is too remote to make him good.

XXXIX
Till now, alone the mighty nations strove;
The rest, at gaze, without the lists did stand;
And threatening France, placed like a painted Jove,
Kept idle thunder in his lifted hand.

XL
That eunuch guardian of rich Holland's trade,
Who envies us what he wants power to enjoy;
Whose noiseful valour does no foe invade,
And weak assistance will his friends destroy.

XLI
Offended that we fought without his leave,
He takes this time his secret hate to shew;
Which Charles does with a mind so calm receive,
As one that neither seeks nor shuns his foe.

XLII
With France, to aid the Dutch, the Danes unite;
France as their tyrant, Denmark as their slave.[118]
But when with one three nations join to fight,
They silently confess that one more brave.

XLIII
Lewis had chased the English from his shore,
But Charles the French as subjects does invite;[119]
Would heaven for each some Solomon restore,
Who, by their mercy, may decide their right.

XLIV
Were subjects so but only by their choice,
And not from birth did forced dominion take,
Our prince alone would have the public voice,
And all his neighbours' realms would deserts make.

XLV
He without fear a dangerous war pursues,
Which without rashness he began before;
As honour made him first the danger chuse,

So still he makes it good on virtue's score.

XLVI
The doubled charge his subjects' love supplies,
Who in that bounty to themselves are kind:
So glad Egyptians see their Nilus rise,
And in his plenty their abundance find.[120]

XLVII
With equal power he does two chiefs create,
Two such as each seemed worthiest when alone;[121]
Each able to sustain a nation's fate,
Since both had found a greater in their own.

XLVIII
Both great in courage, conduct, and in fame,
Yet neither envious of the other's praise;
Their duty, faith, and interest too the same,
Like mighty partners equally they raise.

XLIX
The Prince long time had courted fortune's love,
But once possessed did absolutely reign;
Thus with their Amazons the heroes strove,
And conquered first those beauties they would gain.

L
The Duke beheld, like Scipio, with disdain,
That Carthage, which he ruined, rise once more;
And shook aloft the fasces of the main,
To fright those slaves with what they felt before.

LI
Together to the watery camp they haste,
Whom matrons passing to their children show;
Infants first vows for them to heaven are cast,
And future people bless them as they go.[122]

LII
With them no riotous pomp, nor Asian train,
To infect a navy with their gaudy fears;
To make slow fights, and victories but vain;
But war severely, like itself, appears.

LIII
Diffusive of themselves, where'er they pass,
They make that warmth in others they expect;
Their valour works like bodies on a glass,

And does its image on their main project.

LIV
Our fleet divides, and straight the Dutch appear,
In number, and a famed commander, bold;[123]
The narrow seas can scarce their navy bear,
Or crowded vessels can their soldiers hold.

LV
The Duke, less numerous, but in courage more,
On wings of all the winds to combat flies;
His murdering guns a loud defiance roar,
And bloody crosses on his flag-staffs rise.

LVI
Both furl their sails, and strip them for the fight;
Their folded sheets dismiss the useless air;
The Elean plains could boast no nobler sight,[124]
When struggling champions did their bodies bare.

LVII
Born each by other in a distant line,
The sea-built forts in dreadful order move;
So vast the noise, as if not fleets did join,
But lands unfixed, and floating nations strove.[125]

LVIII
Now passed, on either side they nimbly tack;
Both strive to intercept and guide the wind;
And, in its eye, more closely they come back,[126]
To finish all the deaths they left behind.

LVIX
On high-raised decks the haughty Belgians ride,
Beneath whose shade our humble frigates go;
Such port the elephant bears, and so defied
By the rhinoceros, her unequal foe.

LX
And as the built,[127] so different is the fight,
Their mounting shot is on our sails designed;
Deep in their hulls our deadly bullets light,
And through the yielding planks a passage find.[128]

LXI
Our dreaded admiral from far they threat,
Whose battered rigging their whole war receives;
All bare, like some old oak which tempests beat,

He stands, and sees below his scattered leaves.

LXII
Heroes of old, when wounded, shelter sought;
But he, who meets all danger with disdain,
Even in their face his ship to anchor brought,
And steeple-high stood propt upon the main.[129]

LXIII
At this excess of courage, all amazed,
The foremost of his foes awhile withdraw;
With such respect in entered Rome they gazed,
Who on high chairs the god-like Fathers saw.[130]

LXIV
And now, as where Patroclus' body lay,
Here Trojan chiefs advanced, and there the Greek;
Ours o'er the Duke their pious wings display,
And theirs the noblest spoils of Britain seek.

LXV
Meantime his busy mariners he hastes,
His shattered sails with rigging to restore;
And willing pines ascend his broken masts,
Whose lofty heads rise higher than before.

LXVI
Straight to the Dutch he turns his dreadful prow,
More fierce the important quarrel to decide;
Like swans, in long array, his vessels show,
Whose crests advancing do the waves divide.

LXVII
They charge, recharge, and all along the sea
They drive, and squander the huge Belgian fleet;
Berkley alone, who nearest danger lay,
Did a like fate with lost Creusa meet.[131]

LXVIII
The night comes on, we eager to pursue
The combat still, and they ashamed to leave;
Till the last streaks of dying day withdrew,
And doubtful moonlight did our rage deceive.

LXIX
In the English fleet each ship resounds with joy,
And loud applause of their great leader's fame;
In fiery dreams the Dutch they still destroy,

And, slumbering, smile at the imagined flame.

LXX
Not so the Holland fleet, who, tired and done,
Stretched on their decks, like weary oxen, lie;
Faint sweats all down their mighty members run,
Vast bulks, which little souls but ill supply.

LXXI
In dreams they fearful precipices tread;
Or, shipwrecked, labour to some distant shore;
Or in dark churches walk among the dead;
They wake with horror, and dare sleep no more,

LXXII
The morn they look on with unwilling eyes,
Till from their main-top joyful news they hear
Of ships, which, by their mould, bring new supplies,
And in their colours Belgian lions bear.[132]

LXIII
Our watchful general had discerned from far
This mighty succour, which made glad the foe;
He sighed, but, like a father of the war,
His face spake hope, while deep his sorrows flow.[133]

LXXIV
His wounded men he first sends off to shore,
Never, till now, unwilling to obey;
They, not their wounds, but want of strength, deplore,
And think them happy, who with him can stay.

LXXV
Then to the rest, "Rejoice," said he, "to-day;
In you the fortune of Great Britain lies;
Among so brave a people, you are they,
Whom heaven has chose to fight for such a prize.

LXXVI

"If number English courages could quell,
We should at first have shun'd, not met, our foes,
Whose numerous sails the fearful only tell;[134]
Courage from hearts, and not from numbers grows."[135]

LXXVII
He said, nor needed more to say; with haste,
To their known stations, cheerfully they go;

And, all at once, disdaining to be last,
Solicit every gale to meet the foe.

LXXVIII
Nor did the encouraged Belgians long delay,
But, bold in others, not themselves, they stood;
So thick, our navy scarce could steer their way,
But seemed to wander in a moving wood.

LXXIX
Our little fleet was now engaged so far,
That, like the sword-fish in the whale they fought;[136]
The combat only seemed a civil war,
Till through their bowels we our passage wrought.

LXXX
Never had valour, no not ours before
Done aught like this upon the land or main;
Where, not to be o'ercome, was to do more
Than all the conquests former kings did gain.

LXXXI
The mighty ghosts of our great Harries rose,
And armed Edwards looked with anxious eyes,
To see this fleet among unequal foes,
By which fate promised them their Charles should rise.

LXXXII
Meantime the Belgians tack upon our rear,
And raking chase-guns through our sterns they send;
Close by their fire-ships, like jackals, appear,
Who on their lions for the prey attend.[137]

LXXXIII
Silent, in smoke of cannon, they come on;
Such vapours once did fiery Cacus hide:[138]
In these, the height of pleased revenge is shewn,
Who burn contented by another's side.

LXXXIV
Sometimes from fighting squadrons of each fleet,
Deceived themselves, or to preserve some friend,
Two grappling Ætnas on the ocean meet,
And English fires with Belgian flames contend.

LXXXV
Now, at each tack, our little fleet grows less;
And, like maimed fowl, swim lagging on the main.

Their greater loss their numbers scarce confess,
While they lose cheaper than the English gain.

LXXXVI
Have you not seen, when whistled from the fist,
Some falcon stoops at what her eye designed,
And with her eagerness the quarry missed,
Straight flies at check, and clips it down the wind?[139]

LXXXVII
The dastard crow, that to the wood made wing,
And sees the groves no shelter can afford,
With her loud caws her craven kind does bring,
Who, safe in numbers, cuff the noble bird.

LXXXVIII
Among the Dutch thus Albemarle did fare:
He could not conquer, and disdained to fly;
Past hope of safety, 'twas his latest care,
Like falling Cæsar, decently to die.

LCIX
Yet pity did his manly spirit move,
To see those perish who so well had fought;
And generously with his despair he strove,
Resolved to live till he their safety wrought.

XC

Let other muses write his prosperous fate,
Of conquered nations tell, and kings restored;
But mine shall sing of his eclipsed estate,
Which, like the sun's, more wonders does afford.

XCI
He drew his mighty frigates all before,
On which the foe his fruitless force employs;
His weak ones deep into his rear he bore,
Remote from guns, as sick men from the noise.[140]

XCII
His fiery cannon did their passage guide,
And following smoke obscured them from the foe:
Thus Israel, safe from the Egyptians' pride.
By flaming pillars, and by clouds did go.

XCIII
Elsewhere the Belgian force we did defeat,

But here our courages did theirs subdue;
So Xenophon once led that famed retreat,
Which first the Asian empire overthrew.

XCIV
The foe approached; and one for his bold sin
Was sunk, as he that touched the ark was slain:
The wild waves mastered him, and sucked him in,
And smiling eddies dimpled on the main.

XCV
This seen, the rest at awful distance stood;
As if they had been there as servants set,
To stay, or to go on, as he thought good,
And not pursue, but wait on his retreat.

XCVI
So Libyan huntsmen, on some sandy plain,
From shady coverts roused, the lion chace;
The kingly beast roars out with loud disdain,
And slowly moves, unknowing to give place.

XCVII
But if some one approach to dare his force,
He swings his tail, and swiftly turns him round:
With one paw seizes on his trembling horse,
And with the other tears him to the ground.

XCVIII
Amidst these toils succeeds the balmy night;
Now hissing waters the quenched guns restore;
And weary waves, withdrawing from the fight,
Lie lulled and panting on the silent shore.

XCIX
The moon shone clear on the becalmed flood,
Where, while her beams like glittering silver play,
Upon the deck our careful general stood,
And deeply mused on the succeeding day.

C
"That happy sun," said he, "will rise again,
Who twice victorious did our navy see;
And I alone must view him rise in vain,
Without one ray of all his star for me.

CI
"Yet, like an English general will I die,

And all the ocean make my spacious grave:
Women and cowards on the land may lie;
The sea's a tomb that's proper for the brave."

CII
Restless he passed the remnant of the night,
Till the fresh air proclaimed the morning nigh;
And burning ships, the martyrs of the fight,
With paler fires beheld the eastern sky.

CIII
But now his stores of ammunition spent,
His naked valour is his only guard;
Rare thunders are from his dumb cannon sent,
And solitary guns are scarcely heard.

CIV
Thus far had fortune power, here forced to stay,
No longer durst with fortune be at strife;
This as a ransom Albemarle did pay,
For all the glories of so great a life.

CV
For now brave Rupert from afar appears,
Whose waving streamers the glad general knows;
With full-spread sails his eager navy steers,
And every ship in swift proportion grows.[145]

CVI
The anxious prince had heard the cannon long,
And, from that length of time, dire omens drew
Of English overmatched, and Dutch too strong,
Who never fought three days, but to pursue.

CVII
Then, as an eagle, who with pious care
Was beating widely on the wing for prey,
To her now silent eiry does repair,
And finds her callow infants forced away;

CVIII
Stung with her love, she stoops upon the plain,
The broken air loud whistling as she flies;
She stops and listens, and shoots forth again,
And guides her pinions by her young ones cries.

CIX
With such kind passion hastes the prince to fight,

And spreads his flying canvas to the sound;
Him, whom no danger, were he there, could fright,
Now absent, every little noise can wound.

CX
As in a drought the thirsty creatures cry,
And gape upon the gathered clouds for rain;
And first the martlet meets it in the sky,
And with wet wings joys all the feathered train;

CXI
With such glad hearts did our despairing men
Salute the appearance of the prince's fleet;
And each ambitiously would claim the ken,
That with first eyes did distant safety meet.

CXII
The Dutch, who came like greedy hinds before,
To reap the harvest their ripe ears did yield,
Now look like those, when rolling thunders roar,
And sheets of lightning blast the standing field.

CXIII
Full in the prince's passage, hills of sand,
And dangerous flats, in secret ambush lay;
Where the false tides skim o'er the covered land,
And seamen, with dissembled depths, betray.

CXIV
The wily Dutch, who, like fallen angels, feared
This new Messiah's coming, there did wait,
And round the verge their braving vessels steered,
To tempt his courage with so fair a bait.

CXV
But he, unmoved, contemns their idle threat,
Secure of fame whene'er he please to fight;
His cold experience tempers all his heat,
And inbred worth doth boasting valour slight.

CXVI
Heroic virtue did his actions guide,
And he the substance, not the appearance, chose;
To rescue one such friend he took more pride,
Than to destroy whole thousands of such foes.

CXVII
But when approached, in strict embraces bound,

Rupert and Albemarle together grow;
He joys to have his friend in safety found,
Which he to none but to that friend would owe.

CXVIII
The cheerful soldiers, with new stores supplied,
Now long to execute their spleenful will;
And, in revenge for those three days they tried,
Wish one, like Joshua's, when the sun stood still.

CXIX
Thus reinforced, against the adverse fleet,[146]
Still doubling ours, brave Rupert leads the way;
With the first blushes of the morn they meet,
And bring night back upon the new-born day.

CXX
His presence soon blows up the kindling fight,
And his loud guns speak thick like angry men;
It seemed as slaughter had been breathed all night,
And death new-pointed his dull dart agen.

CXXI
The Dutch too well his mighty conduct knew,
And matchless courage, since the former fight;
Whose navy like a stiff-stretched cord did shew,
Till he bore in, and bent them into flight.

CXXII
The wind he shares, while half their fleet offends
His open side, and high above him shows;
Upon the rest at pleasure he descends,
And, doubly harmed, he double harms bestows.

CXXIII
Behind, the general mends his weary pace,
And sullenly to his revenge he sails;
So glides some trodden serpent on the grass,
And long behind his wounded volume trails.[147]

CXXIV
The increasing sound is borne to either shore,
And for their stakes the throwing nations fear;
Their passions double with the cannons' roar,
And with warm wishes each man combats there.

CXXV
Plied thick and close as when the fight begun,

Their huge unwieldy navy wastes away:
So sicken waneing moons too near the sun,
And blunt their crescents on the edge of day.

CXXVI
And now, reduced on equal terms to fight,
Their ships like wasted patrimonies show;
Where the thin scattering trees admit the light,
And shun each other's shadows as they grow.

CXXVII
The warlike prince had sever'd from the rest
Two giant ships, the pride of all the main;
Which with his one so vigorously he pressed,
And flew so home, they could not rise again.

CXVIII
Already battered, by his lee they lay;
In vain upon the passing winds they call;
The passing winds through their torn canvas play,
And flagging sails on heartless sailors fall.

CXXIX
Their opened sides receive a gloomy light,
Dreadful as day let into shades below;
Without, grim death rides barefaced in their sight,
And urges entering billows as they flow.

CXXX
When one dire shot, the last they could supply,
Close by the board the prince's main-mast bore:
All three, now helpless, by each other lie,
And this offends not, and those fear no more.

CXXXI
So have I seen some fearful hare maintain
A course, till tired before the dog she lay;
Who, stretched behind her, pants upon the plain,
Past power to kill, as she to get away.

CXXXII
With his loll'd tongue he faintly licks his prey;
His warm breath blows her flix[148] up as she lies;
She, trembling, creeps upon the ground away,
And looks back to him with beseeching eyes.

CXXXIII
The prince unjustly does his stars accuse,

Which hindered him to push his fortune on;
For what they to his courage did refuse,
By mortal valour never must be done.

CXXXIV
This lucky hour the wise Batavian takes,
And warns his tattered fleet to follow home;
Proud to have so got off with equal stakes,
Where 'twas a triumph not to be o'ercome.[149]

CXXXV
The general's force, as kept alive by fight,
Now not opposed, no longer can pursue;
Lasting till heaven had done his courage right;
When he had conquered, he his weakness knew.

CXXXVI
He casts a frown on the departing foe,
And sighs to see him quit the watery field;
His stern fixed eyes no satisfaction show,
For all the glories which the fight did yield.

CXXXVII
Though, as when fiends did miracles avow,
He stands confessed e'en by the boastful Dutch;
He only does his conquest disavow,
And thinks too little what they found too much.

CXXXVIII
Returned, he with the fleet resolved to stay;
No tender thoughts of home his heart divide;
Domestic joys and cares he puts away,
For realms are households which the great must guide.[150]

CXXXIX

As those, who unripe veins in mines explore,
On the rich bed again the warm turf lay,
Till time digests the yet imperfect ore,
And know it will be gold another day;[151]

CXL
So looks our monarch on this early fight,
Th' essay and rudiments of great success;
Which all-maturing time must bring to light,
While he, like heaven, does each day's labour bless.

CXLI

Heaven ended not the first or second day,
Yet each was perfect to the work designed:
God and kings work, when they their work survey,
A passive aptness in all subjects find.

CXLII

In burdened vessels first, with speedy care,
His plenteous stores do season'd timber send;
Thither the brawny carpenters repair,
And as the surgeons of maimed ships attend.

CXLIII

With cord and canvas from rich Hamburgh sent,
His navy's molted wings he imps once more;
Tall Norway fir, their masts in battle spent,
And English oak, sprung leaks and planks restore.

CXLIV

All hands employed, the royal work grows warm;
Like labouring bees on a long summer's day,
Some sound the trumpet for the rest to swarm,
And some on bells of tasted lilies play.

CXLV

With glewy wax some new foundations lay,
Of virgin-combs, which from the roof are hung;
Some armed within doors, upon duty stay,
Or tend the sick, or educate the young.

CXLVI

So here some pick out bullets from the sides,
Some drive old oakum through each seam and rift;
Their left hand does the caulking-iron guide,
The rattling mallet with the right they lift.

CXLVII

With boiling pitch another near at hand,
From friendly Sweden brought, the seams in-stops;
Which well paid o'er, the salt sea waves withstand,
And shakes them from the rising beak in drops.

CXLVIII

Some the galled ropes with dawby marline bind,
Or searcloth masts with strong tarpawling coats;
To try new shrouds, one mounts into the wind,
And one below their ease or stiffness notes.

CXLIX

Our careful monarch stands in person by,
His new-cast cannons' firmness to explore;
The strength of big-corn'd powder loves to try,
And ball and cartridge sorts for every bore.

CL

Each day brings fresh supplies of arms and men,
And ships which all last winter were abroad;
And such as fitted since the fight had been,
Or new from stocks, were fallen into the road.

CLI

The goodly London, in her gallant trim,
The Phœnix-daughter of the vanished old,
Like a rich bride does to the ocean swim,
And on her shadow rides in floating gold.

CLII

Her flag aloft, spread ruffling to the wind,
And sanguine streamers, seem the flood to fire;
The weaver, charmed with what his loom designed,
Goes on to sea, and knows not to retire.

CLIII

With roomy decks, her guns of mighty strength,
Whose low-laid mouths each mounting billow laves;
Deep in her draught, and warlike in her length,
She seems a sea-wasp flying on the waves.

CLIV

This martial present, piously designed,
The loyal city give their best-loved king;
And, with a bounty ample as the wind,
Built, fitted, and maintained, to aid him bring.

CLV

By viewing nature, nature's handmaid, art,
Makes mighty things from small beginnings grow:
Thus fishes first to shipping did impart,
Their tail the rudder, and their head the prow.

CLVI

Some log, perhaps, upon the waters swam,
An useless drift, which, rudely cut within;
And hollow'd, first a floating trough became,
And cross some rivulet passage did begin.

CLVII

In shipping such as this, the Irish kern,
And untaught Indian, on the stream did glide;
Ere sharp-keel'd boats to stem the flood did learn,
Or fin-like oars did spread from either side.

CLVIII
Add but a sail, and Saturn so appeared,
When from lost empire he to exile went,
And with the golden age to Tyber steer'd,
Where coin and commerce first he did invent.

CLIX
Rude as their ships was navigation then;
No useful compass or meridian known;
Coasting, they kept the land within their ken,
And knew no north but when the Pole-star shone.

CLX
Of all, who since have used the open sea,
Than the bold English none more fame have won;
Beyond the year, and out of heaven's high way,
They make discoveries where they see no sun.

CLXI
But what so long in vain, and yet unknown,
By poor mankind's benighted wit is sought,
Shall in this age to Britain first be shewn,
And hence be to admiring nations taught.

CLXII
The ebbs of tides, and their mysterious flow,
We, as art's elements, shall understand;
And as by line upon the ocean go,
Whose paths shall be familiar as the land.

CLXIII
Instructed ships shall sail to quick commerce,
By which remotest regions are allied;
Which makes one city of the universe,
Where some may gain, and all may be supplied.

CLXIV
Then we upon our globe's last verge shall go,
And view the ocean leaning on the sky:
From thence our rolling neighbours we shall know,
And on the lunar world securely pry.

CLXV

This I foretel from your auspicious care,
Who great in search of God and nature grow;
Who best your wise Creator's praise declare,
Since best to praise His works is best to know.

CLXVI

O truly royal! who behold the law,
And rule of beings in your Maker's mind;
And thence, like limbecs, rich ideas draw,
To fit the levelled use of human-kind.

CLXVII

But first the toils of war we must endure,
And from the injurious Dutch redeem the seas;
War makes the valiant of his right secure,
And gives up fraud to be chastised with ease.

CLXVIII

Already were the Belgians on our coast,
Whose fleet more mighty every day became
By late success, which they did falsely boast,
And now, by first appearing, seemed to claim.

CLXIX

Designing, subtile, diligent, and close,
They knew to manage war with wise delay;
Yet all those arts their vanity did cross,
And by their pride their prudence did betray.

CLXX

Nor staid the English long; but, well supplied,
Appear as numerous as the insulting foe;
The combat now by courage must be tried,
And the success the braver nation show.

CLXXI

There was the Plymouth squadron now come in,
Which in the Straits last winter was abroad;
Which twice on Biscay's working bay had been,
And on the midland sea the French had awed.

CLXXII

Old expert Allen, loyal all along,
Famed for his action on the Smyrna fleet;
And Holmes, whose name shall live in epic song,
While music numbers, or while verse has feet.

CLXXIII

Holmes, the Achates of the general's fight,
Who first bewitched our eyes with Guinea gold;
As once old Cato, in the Roman sight,
The tempting fruits of Afric did unfold.

CLXXIV

With him went Spragge, as bountiful as brave,
Whom his high courage to command had brought;
Harman, who did the twice-fired Harry save,
And in his burning ship undaunted fought.

CLXXV

Young Hollis on a muse by Mars begot,
Born, Cæsar-like, to write and act great deeds;
Impatient to revenge his fatal shot,
His right hand doubly to his left succeeds.

CLXXVI

Thousands were there in darker fame that dwell,
Whose deeds some nobler poem shall adorn;
And, though to me unknown, they sure fought well,
Whom Rupert led, and who were British born.

CLXXVII

Of every size an hundred fighting sail;
So vast the navy now at anchor rides,
That underneath it the pressed waters fail,
And with its weight it shoulders off the tides.

CLXXVIII

Now, anchors weighed, the seamen shout so shrill,
That heaven and earth, and the wide ocean, rings;
A breeze from westward waits their sails to fill,
And rests in those high beds his downy wings.

CLXXIX

The wary Dutch this gathering storm foresaw,
And durst not bide it on the English coast;
Behind their treacherous shallows they withdraw,
And there lay snares to catch the British host.

CLXXX

So the false spider, when her nets are spread,
Deep ambushed in her silent den does lie,
And feels far off the trembling of her thread,
Whose filmy cord should bind the struggling fly;

CLXXXI

Then, if at last she find him fast beset,
She issues forth, and runs along her loom;
She joys to touch the captive in her net,
And drag the little wretch in triumph home.

CLXXXII
The Belgians hoped, that, with disordered haste,
Our deep-cut keels upon the sands might run;
Or, if with caution leisurely were past,
Their numerous gross might charge us one by one.

CLXXXIII
But with a fore-wind pushing them above,
And swelling tide that heaved them from below,
O'er the blind flats our warlike squadrons move,
And with spread sails to welcome battle go.

CLXXXIV
It seemed as there the British Neptune stood,
With all his hosts of waters at command;
Beneath them to submit the officious flood,
And with his trident shoved them off the sand.

CLXXXV
To the pale foes they suddenly draw near,
And summon them to unexpected fight:
They start like murderers when ghosts appear,
And draw their curtains in the dead of night.

CLXXXVI
Now van to van the foremost squadrons meet,
The midmost battles hastening up behind;
Who view far off the storm of falling sleet,
And hear their thunder rattling in the wind.

CLXXXVII
At length the adverse admirals appear,
The two bold champions of each country's right;
Their eyes describe the lists as they come near,
And draw the lines of death before they fight.

CLXXXVIII
The distance judged for shot of every size,
The linstocks touch, the ponderous ball expires:
The vigorous seaman every port-hole plies,
And adds his heart to every gun he fires!

CLXXXIX

Fierce was the fight on the proud Belgians' side,
For honour, which they seldom sought before;
But now they by their own vain boasts were tied,
And forced, at least in shew, to prize it more.

CXC
But sharp remembrance on the English part,
And shame of being matched by such a foe,
Rouse conscious virtue up in every heart,
And seeming to be stronger, makes them so.[172]

CXCI
Nor long the Belgians could that fleet sustain,
Which did two generals' fates, and Cæsar's bear;
Each several ship a victory did gain,
As Rupert or as Albemarle were there.

CXCII
Their battered admiral too soon withdrew,
Unthanked by ours for his unfinished fight;
But he the minds of his Dutch masters knew,
Who called that providence, which we called flight.

CXCIII
Never did men more joyfully obey,
Or sooner understood the sign to fly;
With such alacrity they bore away,
As if, to praise them, all the States stood by.

CXCIV
O famous leader of the Belgian fleet,
Thy monument inscribed such praise shall wear,
As Varro, timely flying, once did meet,
Because he did not of his Rome despair.[173]

CXCV
Behold that navy, which, a while before,
Provoked the tardy English close to fight;
Now draw their beaten vessels close to shore,
As larks lie dared, to shun the hobbies'[174] flight.

CXCVI
Whoe'er would English monuments survey,
In other records may our courage know;
But let them hide the story of this day,
Whose fame was blemished by too base a foe.

CXCVII

Or if too busily they will inquire
Into a victory, which we disdain;
Then let them know, the Belgians did retire,
Before the patron saint of injured Spain.[175]

CXCVIII
Repenting England this revengeful day
To Philip's manes[176] did an offering bring;
England, which first, by leading them astray,
Hatched up rebellion to destroy her king.

CXCIX

Our fathers bent their baneful industry,
To check a monarchy that slowly grew;
But did not France or Holland's fate foresee,
Whose rising power to swift dominion flew.

CC
In fortune's empire blindly thus we go,
And wander after pathless destiny;
Whose dark resorts since prudence cannot know,
In vain it would provide for what shall be.

CCI
But whate'er English to the blessed shall go,
And the fourth Harry or first Orange meet;
Find him disowning of a Bourbon foe,
And him detesting a Batavian fleet.[177]

CCII
Now on their coasts our conquering navy rides,
Way-lays their merchants, and their land besets;
Each day new wealth without their care provides;
They lie asleep with prizes in their nets.

CCIII
So close behind some promontory lie
The huge leviathans to attend their prey;
And give no chace, but swallow in the fry,
Which through their gaping jaws mistake the way.

CCIV
Nor was this all; in ports and roads remote,
Destructive fires among whole fleets we send;
Triumphant flames upon the water float,
And out-bound ships at home their voyage end.[178]

CCV

Those various squadrons, variously designed,
Each vessel freighted with a several load,
Each squadron waiting for a several wind,
All find but one,--to burn them in the road.

CCVI

Some bound for Guinea, golden sand to find,
Bore all the gauds the simple natives wear;
Some for the pride of Turkish courts designed,
For folded turbans finest Holland bear.

CCVII

Some English wool vexed in a Belgian loom,
And into cloth of spongy softness made,
Did into France, or colder Denmark, doom,
To ruin with worse ware our staple trade.

CCVIII

Our greedy seamen rummage every hold,
Smile on the booty of each wealthier chest;
And, as the priests who with their gods make bold,
Take what they like, and sacrifice the rest.

CCIX

But ah! how insincere are all our joys!
Which sent from heaven, like lightning, make no stay;
Their palling taste the journey's length destroys,
Or grief, sent post, o'ertakes them on the way.

CCX

Swelled with our late successes on the foe,
Which France and Holland wanted power to cross,
We urge an unseen fate to lay us low,
And feed their envious eyes with English loss.

CCXI

Each element his dread command obeys,
Who makes or ruins with a smile or frown;
Who, as by one he did our nation raise,
So now he with another pulls us down.

CCXII

Yet London, empress of the northern clime,
By an high fate thou greatly didst expire;
Great as the world's, which, at the death of time,
Must fall, and rise a nobler frame by fire.[179]

CCXIII

As when some dire usurper heaven provides,
To scourge his country with a lawless sway;
His birth, perhaps, some petty village hides,
And sets his cradle out of fortune's way:

CCXIV

Till fully ripe his swelling fate breaks out,
And hurries him to mighty mischiefs on;
His prince, surprised at first, no ill could doubt,
And wants the power to meet it when 'tis known:

CCXV

Such was the rise of this prodigious fire,
Which in mean buildings first obscurely bred,
From thence did soon to open streets aspire,
And straight to palaces and temples spread.

CCXVI

The diligence of trades and noiseful gain,
And luxury more late, asleep were laid;
All was the night's; and, in her silent reign,
No sound the rest of nature did invade.

CCXVII

In this deep quiet, from what source unknown,
Those seeds of fire their fatal birth disclose;
And, first, few scattering sparks about were blown,
Big with the flames that to our ruin rose.

CCXVIII

Then in some close-pent room it crept along,
And, smouldering as it went, in silence fed;
Till th' infant monster, with devouring strong,
Walked boldly upright with exalted head.

CCXIX

Now, like some rich or mighty murderer,
Too great for prison, which he breaks with gold;
Who fresher for new mischiefs does appear,
And dares the world to tax him with the old:

CCXX

So 'scapes the insulting Fire his narrow jail,
And makes small outlets into open air;
There the fierce winds his tender force assail,
And beat him downward to his first repair.

CCXXI

The winds, like crafty courtezans, with-held
His flames from burning, but to blow them more;
And, every fresh attempt, he is repelled
With faint denials, weaker than before.[180]

CCXXII

And now, no longer letted of his prey,
He leaps up at it with enraged desire;
O'erlooks the neighbours with a wide survey,
And nods at every house his threatning fire.

CCXXIII

The ghosts of traitors from the bridge descend,
With bold fanatic spectres to rejoice;
About the fire into a dance they bend,
And sing their sabbath notes with feeble voice.[181]

CCXXIV

Our guardian angel saw them where they sate,
Above the palace of our slumbering king;
He sighed, abandoning his charge to fate,
And, drooping, oft looked back upon the wing.

CCXXV

At length the crackling noise and dreadful blaze
Called up some waking lover to the sight;
And long it was ere he the rest could raise,
Whose heavy eyelids yet were full of night.

CCXXVI

The next to danger, hot pursued by fate,
Half-clothed, half-naked, hastily retire;
And frighted mothers strike their breasts too late,
For helpless infants left amidst the fire.

CCXXVII

Their cries soon waken all the dwellers near;
Now murmuring noises rise in every street;
The more remote run stumbling with their fear,
And in the dark men jostle as they meet.

CCXXVIII

So weary bees in little cells repose;
But if night-robbers lift the well-stored hive,
An humming through their waxen city grows,
And out upon each other's wings they drive.

CCXXIX

Now streets grow thronged, and busy as by day;
Some run for buckets to the hallowed quire;
Some cut the pipes, and some the engines play,
And some, more bold, mount ladders to the fire.

CCXXX

In vain; for from the east a Belgian wind
His hostile breath through the dry rafters sent;
The flames, impelled, soon left their foes behind,
And forward with a wanton fury went.

CCXXXI

A key of fire ran all along the shore,
And lightened all the river with a blaze;[182]
The wakened tides began again to roar,
And wondering fish in shining waters gaze.

CCXXXII

Old father Thames raised up his reverend head,
But feared the fate of Simois would return;[183]
Deep in his ooze he sought his sedgy bed,
And shrunk his waters back into his urn.

CCXXXIII

The fire, mean-time, walks in a broader gross;[184]
To either hand his wings he opens wide;
He wades the streets, and straight he reaches cross,
And plays his longing flames on the other side.

CCXXXIV

At first they warm, then scorch, and then they take;
Now with long necks from side to side they feed;
At length, grown strong, their mother-fire forsake,
And a new colony of flames succeed.

CCXXXV

To every nobler portion of the town
The curling billows roll their restless tide;
In parties now they straggle up and down,
As armies, unopposed, for prey divide.

CCXXXVI

One mighty squadron with a side-wind sped,
Through narrow lanes his cumbered fire does haste;
By powerful charms of gold and silver led,
The Lombard bankers and the Change to waste.

CCXXXXVII
Another backward to the Tower would go,
And slowly eats his way against the wind;
But the main body of the marching foe
Against the imperial palace is designed.

CCXXXVIII
Now day appears, and with the day the king,[185]
Whose early care had robbed him of his rest;
Far off the cracks of falling houses ring,
And shrieks of subjects pierce his tender breast.

CCXXXIX
Near as he draws, thick harbingers of smoke,
With gloomy pillars, cover all the place;
Whose little intervals of night are broke
By sparks, that drive against his sacred face.

CCXL
More than his guards his sorrows made him known,
And pious tears, which down his cheeks did shower;
The wretched in his grief forgot their own,
So much the pity of a king has power.

CCXLI
He wept the flames of what he loved so well,
And what so well had merited his love;
For never prince in grace did more excel,
Or royal city more in duty strove.

CCXLII
Nor with an idle care did he behold;
Subjects may grieve, but monarchs must redress;
He chears the fearful, and commends the bold,
And makes despairers hope for good success.

CCXLIII
Himself directs what first is to be done,
And orders all the succours which they bring;
The helpful and the good about him run,
And form an army worthy such a king.

CCXLIV
He sees the dire contagion spread so fast,
That where it seizes all relief is vain;
And therefore must unwillingly lay waste
That country, which would else the foe maintain.

CCXLV

The powder blows up all before the fire;[186]
The amazed flames stand gathered on a heap;
And from the precipice's brink retire,
Afraid to venture on so large a leap.

CCXLVI

Thus fighting fires a while themselves consume,
But straight, like Turks forced on to win or die,
They first lay tender bridges of their fume,
And o'er the breach in unctuous vapours fly.

CCXLVII

Part stay for passage, till a gust of wind
Ships o'er their forces in a shining sheet;
Part creeping under ground, their journey blind,
And climbing from below their fellows meet.

CCXLVIII

Thus to some desert plain, or old wood-side,
Dire night-hags come from far to dance their round;
And o'er broad rivers on their fiends they ride,
Or sweep in clouds above the blasted ground.

CCXLIX

No help avails; for, hydra-like, the fire
Lifts up his hundred heads to aim his way;
And scarce the wealthy can one half retire,
Before he rushes in to share the prey.

CCL

The rich grow suppliant, and the poor grow proud;
Those offer mighty gain, and these ask more;
So void of pity is the ignoble crowd,
When others' ruin may increase their store.

CCLI

As those who live by shores with joy behold
Some wealthy vessel split or stranded nigh;
And from the rocks leap down for shipwrecked gold,
And seek the tempests which the others fly:

CCLII

So these but wait the owners' last despair,
And what's permitted to the flames invade;
E'en from their jaws they hungry morsels tear,
And on their backs the spoils of Vulcan lade.

CCLIII
The days were all in this lost labour spent;
And when the weary king gave place to night,
His beams he to his royal brother lent,
And so shone still in his reflective light.[187]

CCLIV
Night came, but without darkness or repose,
A dismal picture of the general doom;
Where souls, distracted when the trumpet blows,
And half unready, with their bodies come.

CCLV
Those who have homes, when home they do repair,
To a last lodging call their wandering friends;
Their short uneasy sleeps are broke with care,
To look how near their own destruction tends.

CCLVI
Those, who have none, sit round where once it was,
And with full eyes each wonted room require;
Haunting the yet warm ashes of the place,
As murdered men walk where they did expire.

CCLVII
Some stir up coals and watch the vestal fire,
Others in vain from sight of ruin run;
And while through burning lab'rinths they retire,
With loathing eyes repeat what they would shun.

CCLVIII
The most in fields, like herded beasts, lie down,
To dews obnoxious on the grassy floor;[188]
And while their babes in sleep their sorrows drown,
Sad parents watch the remnants of their store.

CCLIX
While by the motion of the flames they guess
What streets are burning now, and what are near,
An infant, waking, to the paps would press,
And meets, instead of milk, a falling tear.

CCLX
No thought can ease them but their sovereign's care,
Whose praise the afflicted as their comfort sing;
E'en those, whom want might drive to just despair,
Think life a blessing under such a king.

CCLXI

Meantime he sadly suffers in their grief,
Outweeps an hermit, and outprays a saint;
All the long night he studies their relief,
How they may be supplied, and he may want.

CCLXII

"O God," said he, "thou patron of my days,
Guide of my youth in exile and distress!
Who me, unfriended, brought'st by wond'rous ways,
The kingdom of my fathers to possess:

CCLXIII

"Be thou my judge, with what unwearied care
I since have laboured for my people's good;
To bind the bruises of a civil war,
And stop the issues of their wasting blood.

CCLXIV

"Thou, who hast taught me to forgive the ill,
And recompense, as friends, the good misled;
If mercy be a precept of thy will,
Return that mercy on thy servant's head.

CCLXV

"Or if my heedless youth has stepped astray,
Too soon forgetful of thy gracious hand,
On me alone thy just displeasure lay,
But take thy judgments from this mourning land.

CCLXVI

"We all have sinned; and thou hast laid us low,
As humble earth, from whence at first we came:
Like flying shades before the clouds we show,
And shrink like parchment in consuming flame.

CCLXVII

"O let it be enough what thou hast done;
When spotted deaths ran arm'd through every street,
With poisoned darts, which not the good could shun,
The speedy could out-fly, or valiant meet.[189]

CCLXVIII

"The living few, and frequent funerals then,
Proclaimed thy wrath on this forsaken place;
And now those few, who are returned again,
Thy searching judgments to their dwellings trace.

CCLXIX
"O pass not, Lord, an absolute decree,
Or bind thy sentence unconditional;
But in thy sentence our remorse foresee,
And in that foresight this thy doom recal.

CCLXX
"Thy threatnings, Lord, as thine, thou may'st revoke;
But, if immutable and fixed they stand,
Continue still thyself to give the stroke,
And let not foreign foes oppress thy land."[190]

CCLXXI
The Eternal heard, and from the heavenly quire
Chose out the cherub with the flaming sword;
And bade him swiftly drive the approaching fire
From where our naval magazines were stored.

CCLXXII
The blessed minister his wings displayed,
And like a shooting star he cleft the night:
He charged the flames, and those that disobeyed,
He lashed to duty with his sword of light.

CCLXXIII
The fugitive flames, chastised, went forth to prey
On pious structures, by our fathers reared;
By which to heaven they did affect the way,
Ere faith in churchmen without works was heard.

CCLXXIV
The wanting orphans saw, with watery eyes,
Their founders' charity in dust laid low;
And sent to God their ever-answered cries;
For he protects the poor, who made them so.

CCLXXV
Nor could thy fabric, Paul's, defend thee long,
Though thou wert sacred to thy Maker's praise;
Though made immortal by a poet's song,
And poets' songs the Theban walls could raise.[191]

CCLXXVI
The daring flames peeped in, and saw from far
The awful beauties of the sacred quire;
But since it was prophaned by civil war,
Heaven thought it fit to have it purged by fire.

CCLXXVII

Now down the narrow streets it swiftly came,
And, widely opening, did on both sides prey;
This benefit we sadly owe the flame,
If only ruin must enlarge our way.

CCLXXVIII

And now four days the sun had seen our woes;
Four nights the moon beheld the incessant fire;
It seemed as if the stars more sickly rose,
And farther from the feverish north retire.

CCLXXIX

In the empyrean heaven, the blessed abode,
The Thrones and the Dominions prostrate lie,
Not daring to behold their angry God;
And an hushed silence damps the tuneful sky.

CCLXXX

At length the Almighty cast a pitying eye,
And mercy softly touched his melting breast;
He saw the town's one half in rubbish lie,
And eager flames drive on to storm the rest.[192]

CCLXXXI

An hollow crystal pyramid he takes,
In firmamental waters dipt above;
Of it a broad extinguisher he makes,
And hoods the flames that to their quarry drove.

CCLXXXII

The vanquished fires withdraw from every place,[193]
Or, full with feeding, sink into a sleep:
Each household genius shows again his face,
And from the hearths the little Lares creep.

CCLXXXIII

Our king this more than natural change beholds;
With sober joy his heart and eyes abound:
To the All-good his lifted hands he folds,
And thanks him low on his redeemed ground.

CCLXXXIV

As when sharp frosts had long constrained the earth,
A kindly thaw unlocks it with cold rain;
And first the tender blade peeps up to birth,
And straight the green fields laugh with promised grain.

CCLXXXV
By such degrees the spreading gladness grew
In every heart which fear had froze before;
The standing streets with so much joy they view,
That with less grief the perished they deplore.

CCLXXXVI
The father of the people opened wide
His stores, and all the poor with plenty fed:
Thus God's anointed God's own place supplied,
And filled the empty with his daily bread.

CCLXXXVII
This royal bounty brought its own reward,
And in their minds so deep did print the sense,
That if their ruins sadly they regard,
'Tis but with fear the sight might drive him thence.

CCLXXXVIII
But so may he live long, that town to sway,
Which by his auspice they will nobler make,
As he will hatch their ashes by his stay,
And not their humble ruins now forsake.[194]

CCLXXXIX
They have not lost their loyalty by fire;
Nor is their courage or their wealth so low,
That from his wars they poorly would retire,
Or beg the pity of a vanquished foe.

CCXC
Not with more constancy the Jews, of old,
By Cyrus from rewarded exile sent,
Their royal city did in dust behold,
Or with more vigour to rebuild it went.[195]

CCXCI
The utmost malice of the stars is past,
And two dire comets, which have scourged the town,
In their own plague and fire have breathed their last,
Or dimly in their sinking sockets frown.

CCXCII
Now frequent trines the happier lights among,
And high-raised Jove, from his dark prison freed,
Those weights took off that on his planet hung,
Will gloriously the new-laid works succeed.[196]

CCXCIII
Methinks already from this chemic flame,
I see a city of more precious mould;
Rich as the town[197] which gives the Indies name,
With silver paved, and all divine with gold.

CCXCIV
Already labouring with a mighty fate,
She shakes the rubbish from her mountain brow,
And seems to have renewed her charter's date,
Which heaven will to the death of time allow.

CCXCV
More great than human now, and more august,[198]
Now deified she from her fires does rise;
Her widening streets on new foundations trust,
And opening into larger parts she flies.[199]

CCXCVI
Before, she like some shepherdess did show,
Who sat to bathe her by a river's side;
Not answering to her fame, but rude and low,
Nor taught the beauteous arts of modern pride.

CCXCVII
Now, like a maiden queen, she will behold,
From her high turrets, hourly suitors come;
The East with incense, and the West with gold,
Will stand like suppliants to receive her doom.

CCXCVIII
The silver Thames, her own domestic flood,
Shall bear her vessels like a sweeping train;
And often wind, as of his mistress proud,
With longing eyes to meet her face again.

CCXCIX
The wealthy Tagus, and the wealthier Rhine,
The glory of their towns no more shall boast;
And Seyne, that would with Belgian rivers join,[200]
Shall find her lustre stained, and traffic lost.

CCC
The venturous merchant, who designed more far,
And touches on our hospitable shore,
Charmed with the splendour of this northern star,
Shall here unlade him, and depart no more.

CCCI
Our powerful navy shall no longer meet,
The wealth of France or Holland to invade;
The beauty of this town, without a fleet,
From all the world shall vindicate her trade.

CCCII
And while this famed emporium we prepare,
The British ocean shall such triumphs boast,
That those, who now disdain our trade to share,
Shall rob like pirates on our wealthy coast.

CCCIII
Already we have conquered half the war,
And the less dangerous part is left behind;
Our trouble now is but to make them dare,
And not so great to vanquish as to find.[201]

CCCIV
Thus to the eastern wealth through storms we go,
But now, the Cape once doubled, fear no more;
A constant trade-wind will securely blow,
And gently lay us on the spicy shore.[202]

John Dryden – A Short Biography

John Dryden was born on August 9th, 1631 in the village rectory of Aldwincle near Thrapston in Northamptonshire, where his maternal grandfather was Rector of All Saints Church.

Dryden was the eldest of fourteen children born to Erasmus Dryden and wife Mary Pickering, paternal grandson of Sir Erasmus Dryden, 1st Baronet (1553–1632) and wife Frances Wilkes, Puritan landowning gentry who supported the Puritan cause and Parliament.

As a boy Dryden lived in the nearby village of Titchmarsh, Northamptonshire where it is probable that he received his first education.

In 1644 he was sent to Westminster School as a King's Scholar where his headmaster was Dr. Richard Busby, a charismatic teacher but severe disciplinarian. Having recently been re-founded by Elizabeth I, Westminster now embraced a very different religious and political spirit encouraging royalism and high Anglicanism but as a humanist public school, it maintained a curriculum which trained pupils in the art of rhetoric and the presentation of arguments for both sides of a given issue. This skill would remain with Dryden and influence his later writing and thinking, as much of it displays these dialectical patterns.

His first published poem, whilst still at Westminster, was an elegy with a strong royalist flavour on the death of his schoolmate Henry, Lord Hastings from smallpox, and alludes to the execution of King Charles I, which took place on January 30th, 1649.

In 1650 Dryden was ready for University and travelled to Trinity College, Cambridge. Dryden's undergraduate years would almost certainly have followed the standard curriculum of classics, rhetoric, and mathematics.

Dryden obtained his BA in 1654, graduating top of the list for Trinity that year.

However family tragedy struck in June of the same year when Dryden's father died, leaving him some land which generated a small income, but not enough to live on.

Returning to London during The Protectorate, Dryden now obtained work with Cromwell's Secretary of State, John Thurloe. This may have been the result of influence exercised on his behalf by his cousin the Lord Chamberlain, Sir Gilbert Pickering.

At Cromwell's funeral on 23 November 1658 Dryden was in the company of the Puritan poets John Milton and Andrew Marvell. The setting was to be a sea change in English history. From Republic to Monarchy and from one set of lauded poets to what would soon become the Age of Dryden.

The start began later that year when Dryden published the first of his great poems, Heroic Stanzas (1658), a eulogy on Cromwell's death which is necessarily cautious and prudent in its emotional display.

With the Restoration of the Monarchy in 1660 Dryden celebrated in verse with Astraea Redux, an authentic royalist panegyric. In this work the interregnum is illustrated as a time of anarchy, and Charles is seen as the restorer of peace and order.

With the king now established Dryden moved quickly to place himself as the leading poet and critic of his day and transferred his allegiances to the new government.

Along with Astraea Redux, Dryden welcomed the new regime with two more panegyrics: To His Sacred Majesty: A Panegyric on his Coronation (1662) and To My Lord Chancellor (1662).

These panegyrics are occasional and written to celebrate events. Thus they are written for the nation rather than the self, but these and others put him in good standing for his eventual appointment as Poet Laureate, where a number of event poems would be required each year and speaking for the Nation and to the Nation would be the first order of duty.

These poems suggest that Dryden was looking to court a possible patron which would have given him an income and time to explore his creative ideas but no, his path instead would be to make a living in writing for publishers, not for the aristocracy, and thus ultimately for the reading public.

In November 1662 Dryden was proposed for membership in the Royal Society, and he was elected an early fellow. However, his inactivity and non payment of dues led to his expulsion in 1666.

On December 1st, 1663 Dryden married the Royalist sister of Sir Robert Howard—Lady Elizabeth Howard (died 1714). The marriage was at St. Swithin's, London, and the consent of the parents is noted on the license, though Lady Elizabeth was then about twenty-five. She was the object of some scandals, well or ill founded; it was said that Dryden had been bullied into the marriage by her brothers. A small estate in

Wiltshire was settled upon them by her father. The lady's intellect and temper were apparently not good; her husband was treated as an inferior by those of her social status.

Dryden's works occasionally contain outbursts against the married state but also celebrations of the same. Little else is known of the intimate side of his marriage.

Both Dryden and his wife were warmly attached to their children. They had three sons: Charles (1666–1704), John (1668–1701), and Erasmus Henry (1669–1710). Lady Elizabeth Dryden survived her husband, but went insane soon after his death and died in 1714.

With the re-opening of the theatres after the Puritan ban, Dryden began to also write plays. His first play, The Wild Gallant, appeared in 1663 but was not successful. From 1668 on he was contracted to produce three plays a year for the King's Company, in which he became a shareholder. During the 1660s and '70s, theatrical writing was his main source of income. He led the way in Restoration comedy, his best-known works being Marriage à la Mode (1672), as well as heroic tragedy and regular tragedy, in which his greatest success was All for Love (1678). Dryden was never fully satisfied with his theatrical writings and frequently suggested that his talents were wasted on unworthy audiences.

Certainly therefore fame as a poet looked more rewarding. In 1667, around the same time his dramatic career began, he published Annus Mirabilis, a lengthy historical poem which described the English defeat of the Dutch naval fleet and the Great Fire of London in 1666. It was a modern epic in pentameter quatrains that established him as the pre-eminent poet of his generation, and was crucial in his attaining the posts of Poet Laureate (1668) and then historiographer royal (1670).

When the Great Plague of London closed the theatres in 1665 Dryden retreated to Wiltshire where he wrote Of Dramatick Poesie (1668), arguably the best of his unsystematic prefaces and essays. Dryden constantly defended his own literary practice, and Of Dramatick Poesie, the longest of his critical works, takes the form of a dialogue in which four characters—each based on a prominent contemporary, with Dryden himself as 'Neander'—debate the merits of classical, French and English drama.

He felt strongly about the relation of the poet to tradition and the creative process, and his heroic play Aureng-zebe (1675) has a prologue which denounces the use of rhyme in serious drama. His play All for Love (1678) was written in blank verse, and was to immediately follow Aureng-Zebe.

On December 18th, 1679 he was attacked in Rose Alley near his home in Covent Garden by thugs hired by fellow poet, John Wilmot, 2nd Earl of Rochester, with whom he had a long-standing conflict. Wilmot was constantly in and out of favour with the King and his own poetry was often bawdy, lewd, even obscene and made fun of the King who would often exile him from Court.

Dryden's greatest achievements were in satiric verse: the mock-heroic Mac Flecknoe, a more personal product of his Laureate years, was a lampoon circulated in manuscript and an attack on the playwright Thomas Shadwell. Dryden's main goal in the work is to "satirize Shadwell, ostensibly for his offenses against literature but more immediately we may suppose for his habitual badgering of him on the stage and in print." It is not a belittling form of satire, but rather one which makes his object great in ways which are unexpected, transferring the ridiculous into poetry. This line of satire continued with Absalom and Achitophel (1681) and The Medal (1682). Other major works from this period are the religious poems Religio Laici (1682), written from the position of a member of the Church of England; his 1683 edition of Plutarch's Lives, translated From the Greek by Several Hands in which he introduced the word biography to English readers; and The Hind and the Panther, (1687) which celebrates his conversion to Roman Catholicism.

He wrote Britannia Rediviva celebrating the birth of a son and heir to the Catholic King and Queen on June 10th, 1688. When later in the same year James II was deposed in the Glorious Revolution, Dryden's refusal to take the oaths of allegiance to the new monarchs, William and Mary, which left him out of favour at court and he had to leave his post as Poet Laureate. Thomas Shadwell, his despised rival, succeeded him. Dryden, England's greatest literary figure, was now forced to give up his public offices and live by the proceeds of his pen alone.

Dryden was an excellent translator with his own style which brought the ire of many critics. Many felt he would embellish or expand anything he felt short or curt. Dryden did not feel such expansion was a fault, arguing that as Latin is a naturally concise language it cannot be duly represented by a comparable number of words in the much larger English vocabulary. He continued with his task of translating works by Horace, Juvenal, Ovid, Lucretius, and Theocritus, a task which he found far more satisfying than writing for the stage.

In 1694 he began work on what would be his most ambitious and defining work as translator, The Works of Virgil (1697), which was published by subscription. The publication of the translation of Virgil was a national event and brought Dryden the sum of £1,400.

His final translations appeared in the volume Fables Ancient and Modern (1700), a series of episodes from Homer, Ovid, and Boccaccio, as well as modernised adaptations from Geoffrey Chaucer interspersed with Dryden's own poems. As a translator, he made great literary works in the older languages available to readers of English.

John Dryden died on May 12th, 1700, and was initially buried in St. Anne's cemetery in Soho, before being exhumed and reburied in Westminster Abbey ten days later. He was the subject of poetic eulogies, such as Luctus Brittannici: or the Tears of the British Muses; for the Death of John Dryden, Esq. (London, 1700), and The Nine Muses.

He is seen as dominating the literary life of Restoration England to such a point that the period came to be known in literary circles as the Age of Dryden. Walter Scott called him "Glorious John."

Dryden was the dominant literary figure and influence of his age. He established the heroic couplet as a standard form of English poetry by writing successful satires, religious pieces, fables, epigrams, compliments, prologues, and plays with it; he also introduced the alexandrine and triplet into the form. In his poems, translations, and criticism, he established a poetic diction appropriate to the heroic couplet—Auden referred to him as "the master of the middle style"—that was a model for his contemporaries and for much of the 18th century. The considerable loss felt by the English literary community at his death was evident in the elegies written about him. Dryden's heroic couplet went on to become the dominant poetic form of the 18th century.

What Dryden achieved in his poetry was neither the emotional excitement of the early nineteenth-century romantics nor the intellectual complexities of the metaphysicals. Although he uses formal structures such as heroic couplets, he tried to recreate the natural rhythm of speech, and he knew that different subjects need different kinds of verse. In his preface to Religio Laici he says that "the expressions of a poem designed purely for instruction ought to be plain and natural, yet majestic... The florid, elevated and figurative way is for the passions; for (these) are begotten in the soul by showing the objects out of their true proportion.... A man is to be cheated into passion, but to be reasoned into truth."

Perhaps the following illustrates Dryden and his life—"The way I have taken, is not so streight as Metaphrase, nor so loose as Paraphrase: Some things too I have omitted, and sometimes added of my own. Yet the omissions I hope, are but of Circumstances, and such as wou'd have no grace in English; and the Addition, I also hope, are easily deduc'd from Virgil's Sense. They will seem (at least I have the Vanity to think so), not struck into him, but growing out of him".

John Dryden – A Concise Bibliography

Astraea Redux, 1660
The Wild Gallant (comedy), 1663
The Indian Emperour (tragedy), 1665
Annus Mirabilis (poem), 1667
The Enchanted Island (comedy), 1667, with William D'Avenant from Shakespeare's The Tempest
Secret Love, or The Maiden Queen, 1667
An Essay of Dramatick Poesie, 1668
An Evening's Love (comedy), 1668
Tyrannick Love (tragedy), 1669
The Conquest of Granada, 1670
The Assignation, or Love in a Nunnery, 1672
Marriage à la mode, 1672
Amboyna, or the Cruelties of the Dutch to the English Merchants, 1673
The Mistaken Husband (comedy), 1674
Aureng-zebe, 1675
All for Love, 1678
Oedipus (heroic drama), 1679, an adaptation with Nathaniel Lee of Sophocles' Oedipus
Absalom and Achitophel, 1681
The Spanish Fryar, 1681
Mac Flecknoe, 1682
The Medal, 1682
Religio Laici, 1682
To the Memory of Mr. Oldham, 1684
Threnodia Augustalis, 1685
The Hind and the Panther, 1687
A Song for St. Cecilia's Day, 1687
Britannia Rediviva, 1688, written to mark the birth of a Prince of Wales.
Amphitryon, 1690
Don Sebastian (play), 1690
Creator Spirit, by whose aid, 1690. Translation of Rabanus Maurus' Veni Creator Spiritus
King Arthur, 1691
Cleomenes, 1692
The Art of Satire, 1693
Love Triumphant, 1694

The Works of Virgil, 1697
Alexander's Feast, 1697
Fables, Ancient and Modern, 1700